MW00723798

WE DID THAT!

Stories of Black Achievement, Perseverance, And Excellence

Marc A. Alexander, Maureen B. Harris

ISBN (Print) 978-1-54391-025-4 (Ebook) 978-1-54390-9579

Foreword

by Mattie Isaac

We Did That is a book of historical stories that are not well known and are not just about African Americans but people of African heritage all over the world. The legends in this book are mostly unheard of; however, they hold significance and value. This book was made to inspire readers, young and old, to not only seek more knowledge but to use that knowledge to make a difference. *We Did That* focuses on all areas of life, and the content could easily be the basis for school projects. As a middle school student, who carries a lot in her backpack, I am particularly pleased that this book is portable.

We Did That instills pride in African Americans who had no prior knowledge or understanding of the past accomplishments recorded in this book. Today, young African Americans need examples to look up to and to be motivated by. Seeing my grandmother and my uncle write this book gives me hope for my own writing career. Just moseying through the stories in We Did That makes me realize just how much my people have really achieved. The authors of this timely book made it for the sole purpose of encouraging its readers and showing them more about their past. They hope that after reading this book, African American children and adults will delve into more of their history. The authors are sharing the experiences and struggles of a mighty people whose stories have yet to be told.

Mattie E. Isaac
March 21, 2017

Foreword

by Marc Alexander

The one hundred plus stories in this book are like people crossing from the dark bondage of obscurity into the bright sunshine of acknowledgment. We have assisted these inventors, educators, politicians, business people, and freedom fighters by bringing their phenomenal struggles and triumphs forward to be woven into the American story as they should have been all along.

Black History has been conspicuously absent from the American story since the story began. Our truths have been separated and relegated to one month a year when their discussion begins and ends in 28 days. America would not be the great nation it is without the brilliance and sacrifice of these formerly unknown heroes and sheroes. It is our hope that the information in this book be a starting point for a deeper search into these people, places, and events.

Marc A. Alexander
March 21, 2017

Table of Contents

ARTS

The Arts encompass not only the visual arts but also the performing arts. As you will see throughout this book, Black people of the world have excelled and continue to excel in the arts. We strive to cite some of the artists who have beautified our world either through the creation of their hands, the movement of their bodies, or through the beliefs of their hearts, and who have remained relatively unknown and unrecognized to the average citizen. **Mo**

In 1956, while visiting the North Carolina Museum of Art, **Ernie Barnes** (1938 - 2009) asked where he might find artwork created by Black artists. He was told by the docent, "Your people don't express themselves that way." Little did this misinformed person realize that his words would become the impetus for one of America's premier artists. Twenty-two years later, Barnes returned to that same museum for a successful solo exhibit of his art.

Barnes first made himself known with the pigskin on the football field and was originally drafted by The Washington Redskins in 1959. He was dropped when they realized that he was a Negro. He was chosen in the 10th round by the then champion Baltimore Colts but was released from training camp; subsequently, he was picked up by the NY Titans where he asked to be released because of safety concerns. He played for the San Diego Chargers, the Denver Broncos and finally the Canadian Football League. In 1965, it was NY Jets owner, Sonny Werblin who realized that Barnes had more worth in front of a canvas than on a football field.

Among his many accomplishments are the five official posters created for the 1984 summer Olympic Games in LA; a series of paintings, entitled *The Beauty of the Ghetto*; a painting of the 1987 champion LA Lakers, entitled *Fastbreak*, and a 1996 painting commissioned to commemorate the 50th anniversary of the NBA, entitled *The Dream Unfolds*. In 2004, Barnes was named *America's Best Painter of Sports* by the American Sport Art Museum and Archives.

Chicago native, **Charles Wilbert White** (1918 - 1979) became interested in art when his mother left him at the main branch of the public library, which was situated in close proximity to The Art Institute of Chicago, while she went shopping. As a result of his talent and his early exposure to art masterpieces, White won three scholarships, two of which were rescinded when they found out that he was a Negro. The third time was the charm for White, however, and he was able to attend the Chicago Art Institute. After finishing the Institute, White was unemployed and wondering how he would support himself. Along came an opportunity with the Work Projects Administration, where White worked for three years. White was always interested in the plight of his people, and his paintings are infused with that theme: scenes of African-American history in the United States, socio-economic struggles, human relationships, and portraits. White's work has been exhibited at many of the major galleries throughout the world.

Romare Howard Bearden (1911 - 1988) was born in Charlotte, NC, educated in Pittsburgh, PA, and was graduated from NYU in 1935. He also studied Art History at Sorbonne in 1950. Bearden's early works consisted of paintings depicting the African American southern experience. The work for which he is best known came later in his career, collages, made from photographs ripped or torn from magazines. His work appeared on the covers of Fortune and Time magazines. The subject of this later work still focused on the African American experience, but it included the Harlem experience, train travel, southern conjure women, jazz and blues musicians. Bearden also designed costumes and sets for the Alvin Ailey American Dance Theater, and programs, sets and designs for Nanette Bearden's Contemporary Dance Theatre.

Joan Bacchus Maynard (August 29, 1928 - January 22, 2006) was a writer and penciller for the Golden Legacy line of history comics. Joan's parents, John and Julia Cooper, told her stories about the plight of blacks. After graduating from Empire State College of the State University of New York, Joan worked as a commercial artist for McGraw-Hill and other companies. In addition to the work that she did with comic books, she also drew covers for Crisis, the magazine of the National Association for the Advancement of Colored People. In addition to her artwork, Joan is best known for her efforts in preserving the historic black settlement Weeksville in Brooklyn.

James Van Der Zee (1886 - 1983), a leading figure in the Harlem Renaissance, is best known for his portraits of Black New Yorkers, particularly the Black middle class. His national prominence came about when his 75,000 pictures depicting a period of six decades of African American life were discovered by the Metropolitan Museum of Art. His carefully signed and dated pictures were known for bringing the spirit of Harlem to life. Van Der Zee experienced a resurgence when art gallery director Donna Mussenden began to structure his home space and organize

3

public appearances for him. They married in 1978, and he became a sought after photographer for a new round of celebrities, including Bill Cosby, Cicely Tyson, Lou Rawls and Jean Michael Basquiat.

MARC - Black artists and their art were shaped and limited by the racism that Blacks faced in the rest of their lives. Black artists were told that Black people didn't have the emotional depth to express themselves through the arts. Limited resources, lack of opportunities, and lack of recognition are issues that have continued to plague Black artists until today.

Norma Merrick Sklarek, a pioneer in the field of architecture, was the first registered black female architect in New York. In 1962, she became the first black female licensed architect in California. In 1990, she became the only black woman elected to the American Institute of Architecture (AIA) College of Fellows. Among her many prominent designs, her best known projects are Terminal One at Los Angeles International Airport (LAX) and the U. S. Embassy building in Tokyo, Japan.

Myra Lillian Davis Hemmings (1895 - 1968) was born in Gonzales, Texas. She graduated from high school in San Antonio, Texas, and attended Howard University in Washington, DC. While at Howard in 1912, Davis and seven others were initiated into the Alpha chapter of the Alpha Kappa Alpha sorority, and Davis became president. After becoming dissatisfied with the AKAs' priorities, Davis and twenty-two other sorors left AKA and founded Delta Sigma Theta sorority. Davis later became the Delta's first president of their Alpha chapter at Howard University. After graduating from Howard in 1913, Davis returned to San Antonio to teach English and drama. She and her husband, actor John Hemmings founded the Phyllis Wheatley Dramatic Guild Players, and Myra starred in three films.

Carl T. Rowan (1925-2000), the first black deputy Secretary of State, was an author, a reporter and a broadcaster. As a boy in Tennessee, Rowan and his four siblings lived in a home with no electricity, running water, telephone or a clock. As if the lack of amenities was not enough, Carl was not even allowed to check out books from the public library. Despite all of these hardships, Carl graduated at the top of his class. He went on to earn a Bachelor's degree from Oberlin College and a Master's from the University of Minnesota. After obtaining a reporting job at the Minneapolis Tribune, Rowan was given assignments all over the world. V-P Lyndon B. Johnson noticed Rowan's reporting and appointed him to a job in the State Department. After leaving the Federal government in 1965, Rowan wrote a syndicated column and broadcasted radio commentaries.

Ivan Dixon (1931 - 2008) an American actor, director, and producer, was raised in Harlem on the same block with Josh White, Ralph Ellison and the Hines brothers. He is probably best known for his series role as James (Ivan) "Kinch" Kinchloe in the 1960s sitcom *Hogan's Heroes* and for directing many episodes of the television series. Dixon also directed episodes of *The Waltons, the Bionic Woman,* and *Magnum P.I.,* to name a few. Active in the civil rights movement since 1961, Dixon repeatedly refused to take roles that he felt were stereotypical in nature. He served as president of Negro Actors for Action and directed the films *Trouble Man* and *The Spook Who Sat by the Door*, a controversial movie about the first African American CIA agent who turned revolutionary. This film was quickly banned in theaters but now exists in DVD form.

In 1973, **Lonne Elder**, III (1927 - 1996), along with **Suzanne dePasse** (1947-) were the first African Americans to be nominated for Academy Awards for writing--Elder for the screenplay for *Sounder* and dePasse for the script to *Lady Sings the Blues*. Elder, who has a number of well- known writing accomplishments, including: (play) *Ceremonies in Dark Old Men*, for which he was nominated for the Pulitzer Prize, (screenplay) *Bustin' Loose*, and (TV) *A Woman Called Moses*, was born in Americus, GA, but grew up in New Jersey. dePasse, who has among her accomplishments, the discovery of the Jackson Five, serving as president of Motown, and numerous Emmy awards, was born and raised in Harlem.

By producing the "The Homesteader" in 1920, Oscar Micheaux (1884-1951) became the first African American to produce a feature length film. Born in Metropolis, Illinois, on January 2, 1884, he is regarded as the first major African-American feature filmmaker and the most success-ful African-American filmmaker of the first half of the twentieth century. Micheaux, who decided to concentrate on writing, eventually turned to filmmaking, a new industry at the time. He wrote seven novels In 1913, and 1,000 copies of his first book, *The Conquest: The Story of a Negro Homesteader*, were printed. Micheaux's films came about during a time of great change in the African American community. His films featured contemporary black life and dealt with racial relationships between blacks and whites and with blacks trying to achieve success in the larger society. The Oscar Micheaux Society at Duke University continues to honor his work and educate the public about his legacy.

After being named president of the ABC Entertainment Group, **Channing Dungey,** born in 1969 or 1970, became the first African-American to lead a major broadcast network. As an employee of ABC Studios, Dungey, who was born in Sacramento, California, was responsible for overseeing the development of shows, among which are *Scandal, How to Get Away with Murder,* and *Criminal Minds*. Dungey, who graduated magna cum laude from the UCLA School of Theater, Film and Television is a founding member and current board member of Step Up, a national nonprofit membership organization dedicated to helping girls from under-resourced communities fulfill their potential.

The Lincoln Motion Picture Company was founded in 1916, the first movie company owned and controlled by Black filmmakers. **Actor Noble Johnson** and his brother George Johnson created this company; Noble became its president, and George was given the responsibility of marketing the films. Lincoln was incorporated and authorized to issue 25,000 shares of common stock in 1917. Because its circulation was limited to Black churches and schools and the few "colored only" theatres, the films that were made by The Lincoln Motion Picture Company were not great financial successes. Among its few releases were films entitled: *The Realization of a Negro's Ambition, A Trooper of Troop K,* and its swan song, *By Right of Birth*.

Before the "red carpet" and its photo ops with women dressed in finery that costs more than the average person's house, there were Black women and men dressed in the best that they could afford to buy, or better yet the best that they could make. Going to the clubs where Blacks were welcomed, dressed in feathers and furs, shoes shining like new money and hair, well-oiled, were the Harlemites, the Chicagoans, the Philadelphians, the Baltimoreans, the DC and Detroit folks, and many more, strutting their stuff, out for a night, finger-poppin', hand-dancin', and sampling some spirits. Sometimes this one night of entertainment might cost a week's salary, but was it worth it? Oh yeah! Mo

Robert McFerrin, Sr. (1921 - 2006) was the first black male soloist at the Metropolitan Opera, just three weeks after Marian Anderson broke the color ban at the Met, and at a time when, in a lot of cities, Black people weren't allowed in public auditoriums. McFerrin who was raised in Memphis, TN, received an undergraduate degree from Chicago Musical College in 1946; then, moved to New York City. In 1949, he appeared in *Aida* with the National Negro Opera Company. He joined the New England Opera Company in 1950. In 1953, McFerrin won the Metropolitan Opera national auditions and became the first black male to join the company. In 1958, McFerrin was contracted to be the singing voice of Porgy in Otto Preminger's film *Porgy and Bess*. He toured internationally as a recitalist and was also active as a teacher.

Cheryl Adrienne Brown Hollingsworth, born in New York City, went to college in Decorah, Iowa. In 1970, while there, she became a contestant in the Miss Iowa beauty pageant and won. She was able to become the first African American contestant in the Miss America pageant because of the abolishment of Rule Seven, which read, "...contestants must be of good health and of the white race." Although Ms. Brown did not win the contest, she opened the door for future African American contestants who did win.

Lois K. Alexander Lane (1916 - 2007) founded the Harlem Institute of Fashion in 1966, and the Black Fashion Museum in 1979. Mrs. Lane received her undergraduate degree from Hampton Institute in 1938, and her Master's degree in retailing, fashion and merchandising from NYU. The research that she did for her Master's thesis led her to the discovery of many little-known African American dressmakers. The site of the Black Fashion Museum in Washington, DC, was selected by Mrs. Alexander because it was formerly the Sojourner Truth Home for Women and Girls. This location has been recognized by the National Park Service as a possible Underground Railroad site.

The World Festival of Black Arts, first held in 1966, in Dakar, Senegal, was the brainchild of then president, Leopold Sédar Senghor. The first Festival Mondial des Arts Negres was an expression of the Negritude movement that endeavored to acknowledge and celebrate the achievements of African people and of African culture throughout the world. This first Festival had attendees from 37 countries, among whom were Duke Ellington, Aimé Césaire, and Josephine Baker. It was not until eleven years later in 1977 that the second, called FESTAC, was held in Lagos, Nigeria. This second event that drew over 17,000 participants from 50 countries, was the largest cultural event ever held on the continent of Africa.

Millie and Christine McCoy (1851 - 1912), conjoined twins who were joined at the lower spine but who each had her own set of arms and legs, were born in Columbus County, NC. The girls and their parents were enslaved by a blacksmith named Jabez McKay. The wife of Joseph Smith, their eventual showman owner, taught the girls to sing, play music and dance, and to recite in German and French. The girls became known as 'The Two Headed Nightingale' and remained popular until they retired in the 1880s.

MARC - Black people to this day struggle with gaining a full and robust representation of all of Black life on TV and in films. After a century of having to accept menial roles that were at best indifferent to the story and at worst being a laughable human prop, the film and TV industry has recently begun to show signs of embracing shows that represent some of the diversity of the Real America.

BUSINESS

All around this country and across the seas, Black people have owned and operated businesses and have made a great deal of money. Unfortunately, their names are not celebrated in the annals of history that grace our classrooms. Even in the Jim Crow South, Blacks founded and created businesses. They struggled and persisted through terror tactics and lack of monetary backing to hold onto something of their own...Mo

Jesse B. Blayton, Sr., (1897-1977) distinguished himself in at least two ways: First, he became the first African-American CPA in Georgia. He went on to become a bank president and a professor at Atlanta University. Secondly, he became the first African American to own and operate a radio station in the United States. Blayton's station, WERD specialized in Negro music that could not be found on any of the other radio stations of that day.

South African businesswoman **Siza Mzimela** became the first black woman to launch her own airline, Fly Blue Crane. The airline, according to Ms. Mzimela, will offer an alternative means of air travel within the Southern African region. Ms. Mzimela also founded an aviation services company, Blue Crane Aviation, that extends consulting, legal and management services to airlines and aviation businesses.

Mellody Hobson (1969 -), Princeton University graduate, is president of the largest African American owned capital investment firm, Ariel Capital Management. She serves as Chair of the Board of Trustees of Ariel Investment Trust and Chair of DreamWorks SKG, Inc. Additionally, Williams has been named to lists of honor by Time Magazine, Ebony Magazine, Working Women's Magazine, World Economic Forum, Esquire and the Wall Street Journal. Actress Vanessa L. Williams' character, Courtney Paige in the television show *The Good Wife* is based on Hobson.

R.Donahue "Don" Peebles (born March 2, 1960) is a real estate entrepreneur, author and political activist. Peebles is the Founder, Chairman and Chief Executive Officer of the Peebles Corporation, the largest African American-owned real estate development and ownership company in the US. He has an estimated 5 billion, 600 square foot portfolio with real estate holdings in New York, Washington, DC, Philadelphia, Boston, Miami and Miami Beach.

In 1978, **Janice Bryant Howroyd** (1952 -) founded the Act-1 Group to help others gain employment. Ms. Howroyd is the first African American woman to own a billion dollar company, and her company that operates in 75 cities across the world has grown to become the largest female minority-owned employment agency in the entire country.

Kenneth Bancroft Clark (1914 - 2005) was the first black president of the American Psychological Association, as well as the first African-American to become a fully tenured professor at the City College of New York. In 1946 he, along with his wife, Mamie Phipps Clark, founded the Northside Center for Child Development and published a report that revealed the psychological effects of school segregation. The report was cited in Brown v. Board of Education. In 1962, Clark helped found Harlem Youth Opportunities Unlimited, a social activism organization designed to increase educational and employment opportunities for Harlem's black youth, as well as to teach Harlem residents how to work with government agencies to their benefit. Kenneth Bancroft Clark also founded Kenneth B. Clark & Associates, a consulting firm concerned with racial issues.

Paul Cuffee (1759-1817) was born in Cuttyhunk, MA, to Kofi, a freed slave and Ruth Moses Slocum, a Wampanoag woman. Cuffee, who was raised in the Quaker tradition, never stopped championing the cause of better conditions for his people. At the age of 19, he sued the Massachusetts courts for the right to vote stating that taxation without representation should be illegal. On his own farm, he built New Bedford's only school for the children of "free Negroes" and personally sponsored their teachers. Cuffe is perhaps best known for his involvement with the effort to relocate freed slaves to Sierra Leone. He helped establish The Friendly Society of Sierra Leone, which provided financial support for the colony.

William T. Shorey (July 13, 1859 – April 15, 1919) was a late 19th-century American whaling ship captain known to his crew as the Black Ahab. He was born in Barbados, but immigrated to Boston in 1875. He became the only black captain operating on the west coast of the United States in the late 1880s and 1890s. Captain Shorey was known for his ability to safely navigate the waters of the Arctic and Pacific Oceans. He retired from whaling in 1908, when the demand for whale products decreased and lived in Oakland until his death during the Spanish flu pandemic in 1919.

Lisa Williams created Circle of Friends and Living Water for Girls, a safe haven for women and girls who have been victimized by violence, on seven acres of property in Georgia. Ms. Williams was compelled to create these programs when she read about a 10 yr old girl prosecuted for prostitution, while the men who used her and made money from her walked free. Ms. Williams, once a victim herself, is determined to help these young women and girls have a better life.

Paula Williams Madison was born in Harlem, New York, in 1952. Madison wanted to become an educator and spent her summers teaching inner-city youth about African-American history. After high school, she received a scholarship to Vassar College, where she majored in Black Studies and graduated with her B.A. degree in 1974. She went on to become an executive vice-president at NBC. Madison was the first African-American woman to become a general manager of a top five network-owned television station. She was also the first person to hold the position of senior vice president of diversity at NBC. Throughout her career Madison has promoted the fair inclusion and representation of minorities in the media. Madison's family owns Williams Group Holdings LLC, which has significant investments in media (The Africa Channel), a sports franchise (the WNBA's Los Angeles Sparks), and various real estate, consumer, financial and trading businesses. In addition to being named chairperson and CEO of the Los Angeles Sparks, she also became a member of the WNBA Board of Governors.

Andrew J. Beard, (1849-1921) born as a slave on a plantation in Woodland, Alabama, became a farmer, carpenter, blacksmith, railroad worker, businessman and inventor. He patented three different plows and raised enough money to go into the real estate business making about $30,000. In 1889, Beard invented a rotary steam engine. While Beard worked on his rotary steam engine, he experimented with perhaps his finest invention, an automatic car coupler. In the early days of American railroading, coupling was done manually and was extremely dangerous. Beard's invention alleviated this problem.

Sarah Gammon Bickford (1855 - 1931) was born into slavery, but after Freedom, she left her North Carolina hometown and went to live with an aunt in Tennessee. At the age of 15, a judge employed her to take care of his children, and she relocated to Virginia City, Montana, along with the family. Bickford married twice; she and her second husband, Stephen Bickford, acquired rights to a portion of the water system that supplied drinking water to Virginia City. After his death in 1900, Sarah assumed control of the water company, but it was not until 1917 that she was able to obtain the final third of the water company. She became, then, the only African American woman in Montana, if not the entire country to own a utility company.

Robert Wedgeworth, the first African American Executive Director of the American Library Association, also became President of ProLiteracy Worldwide in August 2002 when Laubach Literacy International (LLI) and Literacy Volunteers of America, Inc. (LVA) merged. ProLiteracy Worldwide, an adult literacy training organization, is the largest non-governmental literacy training organization in the world. ProLiteracy has affiliates and partner organizations in over 60 developing countries of Africa, Asia, Latin America and the Middle East. In its headquarters in Syracuse, NY, ProLiteracy employs more than 100 staff.

MARC - The second Civil Rights Movement has to be about economics as Black people still struggle with racist hiring practices and the inability to keep our one trillion dollars in spending in our community. Starting and sustaining businesses is the key, and as history has shown, we are more than capable of succeeding in all areas of business.

EDUCATION

Coming out of enslavement and into their right of freedom, our ancestors sought, along with a place to live and a means to earn a living, an education. Having been denied this basic right, they yearned for the ability to read and write. They knew that to continue without these skills, they would remain in darkness, similar to what they had experienced in slavery. They recognized that without that piece of the "freedom" pie, they would continue to be used, tricked and cheated by their former enslavers..Mo

Richard Theodore Greener (1844 - 1922), was born in Philadelphia, Pennsylvania. In 1870, Greener became the first African American graduate of Harvard College. He was appointed principal of Philadelphia's Institute for Colored Youth, which later became Cheyney University. Later, Greener obtained a law degree from the University of South Carolina. He was admitted to the Supreme Court of South Carolina in 1877, and the bar of the District of Columbia the following year. In 1879, Greener was appointed Dean of Howard University's Law Department. Greener became prominent in international affairs and was appointed United States Consul at Bombay, India, in 1898, by President William McKinley. Greener never went to India because of the Bubonic Plague then raging in Bombay.

Dr. Clifton R. Wharton, Jr., born in 1926, distinguished himself in many ways. While attending Harvard College, Wharton became the first black announcer at the campus radio station and the first black secretary of the National Student Association. He later became the first African-American accepted into the School of Advanced International Studies at Johns Hopkins University. Continuing on this prominent path, Wharton became the first black person to sit on the board of one of the ten largest corporations in the United States when he was appointed a director of Equitable Life Assurance Society of the United States. Wharton became the first African American to head a major university when he was appointed as president of the University of Michigan in 1970. In 1978, he was appointed Chancellor of the State University of New York's (SUNY) 64 campuses. He held the position until 1987. Afterward, he was Chairman of the Rockefeller Foundation; CEO of the Teachers Insurance and Annuity Association and the College Retirement Equities Fund (TIAA-CREF); and Deputy Secretary of State in the Administration of President Bill Clinton.

Frederick Douglass Patterson (1901-1988) was born in Washington, DC, and orphaned at the age of two. He went on to earn a PhD in veterinary medicine from Iowa State College at the age of 22 and served as the Director of Agriculture at Virginia State College, as well as teaching veterinary science there. Patterson was second only to Booker T. Washington in being the youngest leader of Tuskegee Institute when, at age 34, he became president of the college. In 1943, Patterson founded the United Negro College Fund (UNCF), a national effort to collectively raise funds for twenty-seven small, private, historically black colleges and universities across the South.

EDUCATION

Edward Bouchet (1852 - 1918), born in New Haven, Connecticut, was the first African-American to earn a PhD from an American university and the first African-American to graduate from Yale University in 1874. Bouchet was also the first African-American to be elected to Phi Beta Kappa (the oldest honor society, founded at the College of William and Mary in 1776). He taught at the Institute for Colored Youth in Philadelphia (later became the first Historically Black College or University, Cheyney State) for more than 25 years.

Dr. Ruth Simmons, who was born July 3, 1945, in Grapeland, Texas, became the first African American woman to head an Ivy League University when she was named president of Brown University. Immediately prior to taking over at Brown, Simmons served as president of another prestigious school, Smith College. In 2002, *Newsweek* selected her as a Ms. Woman of the Year, while in 2001, Time named her as America's best college president. She is a Honorary Member of Alpha Kappa Alpha Sorority, Inc.

Arturo Schomburg (1874 - 1938) was born in Santurce, Puerto Rico. He was a historian, writer, and activist in the United States, who researched and raised awareness of the great contributions that Afro-Latin Americans and African-Americans have made to society. In 1911, Schomburg co-founded with John Edward Bruce the Negro Society for Historical Research, to create an institute to support scholarly efforts. For the first time it brought together African, West Indian and Afro-American scholars.

In 1925, Schomburg wrote an essay, entitled *The Negro Digs up his Past*, a magazine article that inspired many well-known African Americans of that time and continues to be relevant. He was an important intellectual figure in the Harlem Renaissance.

Fanny Jackson Coppin (1837 - 1913) was born enslaved in Washington, DC. At the age of 12, she gained her freedom when she was purchased by her aunt. In 1860, she enrolled in Oberlin College. She graduated with a Bachelor's degree in 1865 and accepted a position at Philadelphia's Institute for Colored Youth (now Cheyney University of Pennsylvania). She served as the principal of the Ladies Department and taught Greek, Latin, and Mathematics. In 1869, Fanny was appointed as the principal of the Institute, becoming the first woman, black or white, to become a school principal. In her 37 years at the Institute, Fanny Jackson was responsible for vast educational improvements at the school. Perhaps her most significant addition to the ICY structure was the vocational-technical department that opened in 1889. Although it did not have the higher level courses that Coppin had championed, it was the only vocational school in Philadelphia at the turn of the century.

We have few historic facts about elementary and secondary education for Blacks. Not much has been recorded about the one-room schoolhouse, or the teacher who held sway over the students therein. My mother told me about her experience in such a place in Nottoway County, Virginia, during the 20s and the 30s. She and my father both were taught by a young lady from the neighborhood--a young lady who earned her teaching credentials at a "normal" school, rather than a 4-year college or university. This teacher, my mother told me, made sure

that her students knew more than what was required. Students came to school every day that they could because during harvest time, many students had to stay at home and help, thus falling far behind their class-mates. If the family fell on hard times, education could be over for the 14 year-old student. At that time, there were no behavior problems--that was not a concern for the teacher. Her concern was books, desks, chalk and chalkboards. How different elementary and secondary education is today--especially in our cities. Most teachers have access to decent materials--if not books, then the internet. Most students have somewhere to sit, though not always a desk of their own. In many of our schools there is overcrowding; impossible demands are placed on the teachers who try to teach 35+ students in some elementary classrooms. There are programs, interventions, booster groups and still our Black students lag behind. With all of the progress we have made in education, we still have not discovered how to sell "learning" and "knowing" as the door to the future. We have not yet been able to convince so many of our youth that despite everything that can be taken from them, a well-developed mind is theirs to keep forever...Mo

Nathan Hare was born in the town of Slick, Oklahoma, on April 9, 1933, on a sharecropper's farm. In 1961, he became an instructor and assis-tant professor in sociology at Howard University in Washington, D.C. Some of his students included activist Stokely Carmichael and author Claude Brown. After being dismissed from the faculty at Howard because of phil-osophical differences with the administration, Hare joined the faculty of San Francisco State College (now San Francisco State University) and became the program coordinator of the school's Black Studies program, the first in the United States. This has earned him the title "father of Black Studies" by scholars. As the program coordinator, Hare created the term "ethnic studies" to replace "minority studies." In 1969, he founded the scholarly periodical, *The Negro Scholar: A Journal of Black Studies and Research.* He left this work in 1975 to work as a clinical psychologist in community health programs, hospitals, and in private practice. In 1979, he co-founded the Black Think Tank with his wife, Julia Hare.

Tererai Trent, born in Zimbabwe in 1965, is an African American woman whose unlikely educational success has brought her international fame. Tererai Trent was not allowed to go to school as a child because of poverty and because of her being female. She taught herself to read and write using her brother's books and eventually started doing her brother's homework. In 1991, Jo Luck from Heifer International visited her village and asked every woman about her greatest dream. Tererai Trent said she wanted to go to America and get a bachelor's degree, a master's, and eventually a PhD. In 1998, she moved to Oklahoma with her husband and their five children. Three years later, she earned a bachelor's degree in agricultural education. In 2003, Trent earned her master's degree, and her husband was deported for abuse. She has since remarried, to Mark Trent, a plant pathologist whom she met at Oklahoma State University. After she earned each degree, she returned to Zimbabwe and checked off each goal she accomplished, one by one. In December 2009, she earned her doctorate from Western Michigan University; her thesis looked at HIV/AIDS prevention programs for women and girls in sub-Saharan Africa.

The Jeanes Supervisors (1907- 1968) planted the seeds for education and social change in the deep South. The Jeanes Supervisors were a team of African American teachers who worked in southern rural schools and communities in the United States between 1907 and 1968, allowing African Americans to get an education in these areas. The group, that got its name from Philadelphia philanthropist Anna T. Jeanes, was also known at times as Jeanes Teachers, Supervising Industrial Teachers, or Jeanes Workers. This group gave African American women in the South an opportunity to work, where they otherwise would not have been able to. Jeanes Supervisors provided community self-help, instruction on academic schools subjects and industrial information. In 1951, in Georgia, ninety-five Jeanes Supervisors were being paid by the state; the state, however, was unaware that many Jeanes Supervisors were doing more than just teaching school. Some were members of the NAACP and the Georgia Teachers and Education Association (GTEA), and those Supervisors provided information to African American communities about equal schools and voting rights. By so doing many Supervisors functioned as leaders of the early civil rights movement during the 1950s.

John Hope (1868 - 1936) was born in Augusta, Georgia. After his father's untimely death, Hope was forced to leave school to help support his family; he was, however, able to return to school and graduated from Worcester Academy and Brown University. Hope was the first person of African descent selected to be president of both Morehouse College (1906) and Atlanta University (1929). He worked to develop Atlanta University's graduate programs to ensure higher education for blacks. Hope was active in national civil rights organizations, including the Niagara Movement, the succeeding National Association for the Advancement of Colored People (NAACP), and the Southern based Commission on Interracial Cooperation. In addition, he was active in the National Urban League, the YMCA and the National Association of Teachers in Colored Schools. In 1936, he was awarded the NAACP's Spingarn Medal.

John Berry Meachum (1789-1854) was born into slavery in Goochland Co., Virginia. By the age of 21 he had earned enough money doing carpentry work to purchase his freedom and shortly thereafter, his father's.

While living in Kentucky, Meachum married an enslaved woman who was moved to St. Louis before he had earned enough money to buy her freedom. He followed her to St. Louis to buy her freedom, and while there, Meachum met a white Baptist minister named John Mason Peck. Peck and Meachum soon became allies in creating a worship space for black people, and together they provided a Sunday school and religious services for slaves and free black people in the area.

In 1825, after having been ordained as a Baptist Minister, Meachum founded and became the pastor of First African Baptist Church. In addition to providing space and facilities in which Black people could worship, Meachum and Peck also offered education to the Black people of St. Louis. First African Baptist Church offered education to as many as 300 people who were charged a monthly tuition fee of one dollar, but no one was turned away for being unable to pay. Because St. Louis, which originally backed the education of Blacks as a means to foster Christianity, devised an ordinance to ban the education of free black people, Meachum was forced to disband his educational efforts.

After St. Louis banned all education for Blacks, Meachum turned tables on them and customized a steamboat with a library, desks, and chairs. This steamboat became the Floating Freedom School in the middle of the Mississippi River, outside the reach of Missouri officials. In addition to their education, John and Mary Meachum also helped enslaved people to freedom through the Underground Railroad. By means of the income provided by his successful carpentry business, John Meachum was also able to purchase and free twenty enslaved individuals who he trained in carpentry and other trades so that they could earn a living. In a pamphlet entitled, *An Address To All The Colored Citizens of the United States,* he previewed the philosophy of Booker T. Washington by urging black people to embrace practical, hands-on education so they would be able to support themselves after emancipation.

KELLY MILLER (1863 - 1939), who was born in Winnsboro, SC, earned a B.A. from Howard University in 1886. In 1887, Miller became the first African American graduate student at Johns Hopkins University, where he studied mathematics and physics. Because of financial constraints, Miller had to leave Johns Hopkins. He became a high school mathematics teacher for a short period prior to becoming a math professor at Howard. After introducing sociology into Howard's curriculum, Miller became a sociology professor at Howard. He subsequently earned an M.A. and a law degree from Howard Law School and became dean of the College of Arts and Sciences at Howard. Miller, being a person of great intellect, helped found the first organization for black intellectuals known as the American Negro Academy. The American Negro Academy consisted of persons of African descent from around the world and was the first society of blacks that promoted the "Talented Tenth" philosophy of W.E.B. DuBois, another of its founders. The ANA welcomed males with backgrounds in law, medicine, literature, religion, and community activism. The goal of this organization was to lead their people, protect them, and eradicate racism.

MARC - Many Black achievers have attended HBCUs (Historically Black Colleges and Universities). For nearly a century these small but mighty schools were just about the only option for those who wanted to attend college. A lot of these schools face hard times because alumni donations are low, and they face a government that continues to call into question their viability in an America that claims to be post-racial.

Crispus Attucks Wright (1914 - 2001), the son of a former slave went on to become a multimillionaire and a philanthropist. Wright earned a bachelor's degree in political science at USC, followed by a law degree from the same school in 1938. After serving in the army, he established his law practice on Central Avenue in LA. Because of his race, Wright faced exclusion from the existing bar association, and, as a result, in 1943, he co-founded the John M. Langston Bar Association for African Americans, which continues to this day. Wright, remembering the $50 scholarships that helped him to finance law school, donated $2 million in scholarship money to his alma mater, USC. The money, that at the time was the largest gift ever given to USC by an African American, was to be used to fund the Crispus Attucks Wright Scholarships for minority law students and others dedicated to practice in underserved minority communities.

Pearl L. Stewart (1950-) is the first African American woman to be editor of a daily metropolitan newspaper, the Oakland Tribune. She was appointed in 1992 and remained in the position for one year. She certainly learned something about editing when she was enrolled at Howard University.

Stewart was 16 years old when she began her college career at Howard and went on to be the editor of The Hilltop, Howard's campus newspaper. Ms. Stewart received her bachelor's degree from Howard and a master's degree from American University. As a fellow at Harvard University during the 1990s, Ms. Stewart researched and wrote about race and gender-based discrimination in corporate America. In 2002, while teaching at Florida A&M University, Ms. Stewart founded blackcollegewire.org, a website where 22 HBCU student newspapers have been linked, thus increasing communication among black journalism students.

Think about this: African Americans excel in many areas, one of which is the arts. Some of my friends probably would not have gone to school except for the chance to draw, sing, or play an instrument. The big push now is to close the achievement gap, especially among our Black boys. How many of those Black boys might study harder, pay more attention in class if they knew that they could learn to play a trumpet or design a wood sculpture? How would it be for them to use their natural ability to create and make something that would earn them recognition instead of notoriety, an excellent grade rather than a failure? In the push to create academic excellence, so many of our schools are removing the "hook" that actually might encourage many of our Black children to work towards that goal...Mo

FREEDOM

That old Negro spiritual says, "Oh Freedom, Oh Freedom, Oh Freedom, over me...And before I'd be a slave, I'd be buried in my grave..." In how many Black hearts did that song reside? Those who had come out of the enslaved condition; those who just missed it, and those who sat at the knee of an ancestor and heard tales of it—all could attest to the sentiment that the song expressed. No work, no sacrifice, no situation was too much to prevent their determination to direct their own lives...Mo

MARC - Freedom for Black people in America has been a very fluid concept since the first slave ship arrived over 500 years ago. Most American history would have you believe that Black people were one type of enslaved--sad, miserable, and resigned to a life of deprivation and servitude. Reading the stories in this section, however, lets you in on the fact that Black people thought and acted on getting free in a wide variety of ways. Although some may have started enslaved, it never stopped them from reaching the highest heights of American society.

Amelia Boynton Robinson (1911 - 2015) was born in Savannah, Georgia, at a time when African-Americans (men and women) were being lynched in record numbers. Amelia stayed in the middle of the Civil Rights struggle and rubbed shoulders with prominence during her 104-year lifetime. She knew famous scientist George Washington Carver and worked with civil rights leader Dr. Martin Luther King, Jr. She registered to vote in Alabama in 1934, and was badly beaten and bloodied while trying to cross the Edmund Pettus Bridge in Selma, Alabama, on what has become known as Bloody Sunday. She and her husband, S.W. Boynton worked tirelessly for the cause of voting rights and home ownership. In 1964, she sought a seat in Congress and became the first African American female to run for Congress from Alabama as well as the first African-American woman to run on the Democratic ticket for Congress from the state of Alabama.

Paulette Brown was born on April 28,1951, in Baltimore, Maryland. She was educated in the Baltimore public school system during a time when segregation and educational inequities were the norm in American education. She graduated from Seton Hall Law School and made it a point to evade the low-paying jobs into which new African-American lawyers were steered. Jobs, such as public defenders and legal service were handpicked for African Americans instead of jobs in corporate law. Rather than to begin her career in public service, she started her own law firm, eventually merging it into Brown, Lofton, Childress & Wolfe, New Jersey's largest minority firm. She went on to be elected president of the National Bar Association (NBA), and later served as a municipal court judge in Plainfield, New Jersey. As president of the NBA, Brown led a delegation to monitor the first free and democratic elections in South Africa in 1994. Her career has been one of recognition: "One of the 50 most Influential Minority Lawyers in America; New Jersey Super Lawyer; and Recipient of the Spirit of Excellence Award from the ABA Commission on Racial and Ethnic Diversity. She became president of the American Bar Association in 2015, an organization of over 400,000 lawyers that once did not allow African Americans members.

Stagecoach Mary Fields (1832 - 1914) born in Tennessee, gained her freedom at the end of the Civil War, and left the state first for Montana, via Mississippi and Ohio. Mary was called to Ohio by her childhood friend who was the head of a convent in Toledo, and who had fallen ill. Mary relocated and nursed her friend back to health, and subsequently became the forewoman at the convent. Mary was said to always have with her a pistol and a slug of whiskey and was so confident in her abilities and her place in the community that neither Native Americans nor Whites knew what to make of her. Mary went on to become the first African-American woman employed as a mail carrier in the United States and the second woman to work for the United States Postal Service. Mary never missed a day of work even in Montana's deep snow. If the snow was too deep for her horses, Fields delivered the mail on snowshoes, carrying the sacks on her shoulders.

Constance Baker Motley (1921 - 2005) was born in New Haven, Connecticut, and at the age of 15 she became interested in civil rights after being banned from swimming at a public beach because she was an African-American. When she finished high school she wanted to go to college, but her family couldn't afford it. She took a job as a maid and eventually went to college, starting at Fisk University and graduating from New York University. She then went to Columbia Law School, becoming the first African-American woman to graduate in its history. Her first job as a lawyer was working for the NAACP)s Legal Defense and Educational Fund. While working for the NAACP she became the first African-American woman to argue a case in front of the Supreme Court. She won nine out of ten cases argued before the Court between 1961 and 1963, often staunchly defending the brave freedom fighters who dared to desegregate the South. She went on to be a judge, state senator, and Borough President of Manhattan. President Lyndon B. Johnson appointed Motley to the United States District Court in 1966, making her the first African American woman to hold a Federal Judgeship.

Alice Dunnigan (1906 - 1983) was born in Kentucky at a time when African-Americans were being lynched for offenses without the benefit of judge or jury. At age 14, Alice began her writing career by writing a column for the Owensboro Enterprise. After graduating from the Kentucky Normal and Industrial Institute for Colored Students with a degree in teaching, she began her teaching career. Alice realized that the books she was using to teach her students were nearly lacking any mention of the contributions of African-Americans to American history; she subsequently created and published the Kentucky Fact Sheets. These sheets were collected and formed into a manuscript in 1939, and were finally published in 1982 with the title, The Fascinating Story of Black Kentuckians: Their Heritage and Tradition. Alice left teaching and became a reporter, becoming the first African American woman with White House credentials as well as the first to receive a Capitol press pass. Alice was famous for her persistence in asking President Eisenhower about equal rights for African-Americans, a situation that he ignored for years. She was vindicated somewhat when she was the first reporter that President Kennedy called on when he became President in 1961.

James Forten (1766 - 1842) was born free in Philadelphia, PA. At the age of fifteen, he became a powder boy for the Continental Army during the Revolutionary War. After being held as a prisoner of war for 7 months in

England, he returned to America and resumed his employment as a sail maker. He eventually bought the company which became even more successful, and he employed 40 people. Forten was among those in the City of Brotherly Love who formed, along with Richard Allen, the founder of the AME church, the Convention of Color. This organization advocated the migration of freed Blacks to Canada but opposed the idea of a return to Africa. Other important men of the day who joined Forten and Allen in this venture were Henry Highland Garnet, William Wells Brown and Samuel Cornish. Forten used his wealth and fame to great effect and was an architect of the abolitionist movement believing in and championing freedom and equal rights for African-Americans until his death in 1842.

There were **three publications** that included in their names the words "the colored American." The first: *The Colored American* was a newspaper published by Samuel Cornish, Phillip A. Bell, and Charles Bennett Ray, in New York City from 1837 to 1842.

Originally named *The Weekly Advocate*, *The Colored American*, circulated in free black communities in the northeastern United States and had as its focus the moral, political and social elevation of free colored people and the peaceful abolition of the enslaved.

The second publication, also named *The Colored American*, published in Washington, D.C., by Edward Elder Cooper, from 1893 to 1904, was a weekly newspaper that promoted itself as a national Negro newspaper. A yearly subscription to this publication that generally supported Republicans and favored the views of Booker T. Washington cost $2.00.

The third publication: *The Colored American Magazine*, was first published in 1900 and circulated in New York City and Boston, MA, until 1909. The magazine was founded by Walter Wallace, Jesse W. Watkins, Harper S. Fortune, and Walter Alexander Johnson who created a holding company named The Colored Co-Operative Publishing Company.

Pauline Hopkins was its most dedicated writer from its inception, and she functioned as its editor from 1902 until 1904 when the magazine was taken over by Booker T. Washington. The magazine's aim was to showcase the culture that "free" colored people, particularly those in the middle and upper class, were establishing.

President Abraham Lincoln issued the **Emancipation Proclamation** on September 22, 1862, with an effective date of January 1, 1863. In the Confederate States of America it had little to no effect, and the state of Texas, a slave state did not abide by its provisions at all.

On June 18, 1865, Union General Gordon Granger and 2,000 federal troops arrived on the island of Galveston, Texas, to force the state to comply to the law as stated in the Emancipation Proclamation. They proposed to take over the possession of the state and force the emancipation of its slaves. On June 19, Granger read the Emancipation Proclamation, freeing a colored people who had been freed two years earlier. Today Juneteenth is celebrated across the country by African-Americans as a sort of Independence day.

Mary Ellen Pleasant (1814 - 1904) was born a slave in Virginia but spent her early years in Nantucket, MA. After marrying wealthy, white James Smith, an abolitionist, she and he became conductors on the Underground Railroad. Smith died after about four years, and Mary Ellen married John James Pleasant around 1848. The couple moved to San Francisco, where Mary Ellen opened a restaurant / boarding house and became very wealthy. She campaigned for civil rights, successfully desegregating San Francisco's streetcars and was said to have helped finance John Brown's raid on Harpers Ferry. She died in in 1904 and was said to have covertly amassed a joint fortune once assessed at $30,000,000!

Birmingham Children's March, May 2, 1963, was a day organized in response to Martin Luther King, Jr.'s call to "fill the jails" of the city of Birmingham, Alabama. Many of the adults in the city were reluctant to put their jobs and their lives at stake, but the children made the "call" their mission. Flyers had been distributed in black schools and neighborhoods that said, "Fight for freedom first then go to school," and more than 1000 students gathered at the Sixteenth Street Baptist Church, marched to the downtown area to meet with the Mayor and integrate chosen buildings. Over 1000 children were arrested the first day, and on the second day they were sprayed by high-powered hoses, attacked by dogs, and beaten with batons by the Birmingham Police. This brave protest remained in effect for 2 months until Birmingham city officials yielded to the negative national news coverage and the economic impact on city businesses. They agreed to desegregate city businesses and free all of the children from jail. The Children's Crusade had a significant impact on Birmingham and the Civil Rights Movement all over the nation.

North America's **four major rail networks**: Norfolk Southern, CSX, Union Pacific, and Canadian National all own lines that were built with slave labor. Nearly every rail line built east of the Mississippi River and south of the Mason-Dixon Line before the Civil War was constructed at least partly by slaves. Some of the enslaved were leased from their owners and others were purchased by the railroad industry. The enslaved usually cleared, graded and laid tracks. Enslaved workers frequently appear in annual reports itemized as "hands," "colored hands," "Negro hires," "Negro property" and "slaves." The president of Union Pacific's Memphis, El Paso & Pacific Railroad declared that slaves were the least expensive and most reliable laborers.

More than 3.5 million Africans were captured, enslaved and transported against their will to Brazil during the slavery era--more than to any colony in the Americas. The slave trade was officially outlawed in Brazil in 1831, and still slaves were imported by the thousands for the next 50 years, until on May 13, 1888, Brazil became the last nation in the western hemisphere to abolish slavery. Today, only Nigeria has a larger black population than Brazil.

Pedro Alonso Niño (Alonzo Pietro), who was born in Palos de Moguer, Spain, to Black African Moorish parents, captained the Nina, one of the three ships that was a part of Columbus's voyage in 1492. Niño, who explored the coasts of Africa in his early years, also accompanied Columbus during his third voyage that saw the discovery of Trinidad. In May 1499, Niño and his brothers Luis and Cristóbal de la Guerra, returned to the Indies to make their own exploration. They arrived in Maracapana in the West Indies and explored the islands of Margarita, Coche and Cubagua.

Abdu-l-Rahman Ibrahim Ibn Sori (a.k.a. Abdul-Rahman) was a born in 1762 in the country of what is now Guinea. He was a Muslim prince of the Fulani people, and in 1788, he was reportedly captured in battle and sold into slavery. Ibrahim, who became known as the Prince, was enslaved in The Mississippi Delta. In 1826, a letter that Ibrahim wrote to his family in West Africa was intercepted by local newsman Andrew Marschalk. Marschalk sent a copy to the federal capital in Washington D.C., to the attention of U.S. Senator Thomas Reed. Reed assumed that Ibrahim was a Moor and forwarded the letter to the U.S. Consulate in Morocco. The Sultan of Morocco Abderrahmane, though Ibrahim was not Moroccan, was moved to petition U.S. President John Quincy Adams to give Ibrahim his freedom. Ibrahim was granted his freedom and he was allowed to return to his country, but the stipulations were that he would have to leave his family behind. Ibrahim made a desperate attempt to purchase his family's freedom but was only able to raise half the money needed.

Elizabeth Freeman (1744-1829) born in Massachusetts and known as Mumbet, was among the first black slaves in Massachusetts to file a "freedom suit" and win in court under the 1780 constitution, with a ruling that slavery was illegal. Mumbet, who was one of the cooks in her master's household, overheard a dinner table conversation about the new promises of liberty made in the Sheffield Declaration (1773), the Declaration of Independence (1776), and the Massachusetts Constitution (1780). When the state Supreme Court of Massachusetts upheld Walker's freedom, the ruling was considered to have implicitly ended slavery in the state. Mumbet's eloquent statement concerning freedom: "Any time, any time while I was a slave, if one minute's freedom had been offered to me, and I had been told I must die at the end of that minute, I would."

The Deacons of Defense and Justice, a group formed to protect members of the Congress of Racial Equality from Ku Klux Klan violence, began its mission on July 10, 1964, in Jonesboro, Louisiana, led by Earnest "Chilly

Willy" Thomas and Frederick Douglas Kirkpatrick. Most of the "Deacons" were veterans of World War II and the Korean War. The organization soon expanded to include its first affiliate chapter in nearby Bogalusa, Louisiana, led by Charles Sims, A.Z. Young and Robert Hicks. The Deacons confronted the Klan in Bogalusa, thus forcing the federal government to step in on behalf of the local African-American community. The national attention they obtained as a result of this confrontation also persuaded state and national officials to initiate efforts to neutralize the Klan in that area of the Deep South. The Deacons were not a favorite of traditional civil rights organizations, but they were successful in providing protection for local African Americans who sought to register to vote and for white and black civil rights workers in the area. Because of the strategy and methods that the Deacons used, The FBI soon took notice of them and began an investigation. The investigation was diverted, however, when more influential black power organizations such as US and the Black Panther Party emerged after the 1965 Watts Riot.

A large slave revolt, led by mulatto slave driver, Charles Deslondes took place in New Orleans, Louisiana, in 1811. He led a group of enslaved Africans, many of whom had participated in the Haitian Revolution to march on the city of New Orleans with flags flying and drums beating. The enslaved, armed with pikes, hoes, axes and a few firearms, were well organized and moved as military regimens. As they moved toward New Orleans, increasing their numbers as they marched, they sang Creole protest songs, while plundering plantations and murdering whites. Some estimated that the force ultimately swelled to 300. They fought valiantly until they ran out of ammunition, about 20 miles from New Orleans.

MARC - *Traditional American history would have you believe that there were about three slave revolts and out of those three, none was successful. Though slave revolts weren't common, and slaves knew that an unsuccessful revolt was certain death, slave revolts did happen in America. They happened on plantations and on the boats on their way to this country when the captured didn't even know the horrors that awaited them. Misleading is the popular picture of the docile enslaved accepting his/her position; many took action at the risk of death.*

Gaspar Yanga, known as the "first liberator of the Americas" was born in 1545, on the continent of Africa. He was said to have descended from the royal family of Gabon. He was seized and sold into slavery in Mexico. In 1570, he and a small group of former slaves established their own colony, which they called San Lorenzo de los Negros, where they lived for about 40 years. After being implicated in looting nearby haciendas and kidnapping native women, the Spanish government sent soldier Pedro González de Herrera, along with about 550 Spaniards to get rid of the settlement. The maroons, however, fled into the surrounding terrain, which they knew well, and the Spaniards were unsuccessful in their attempt. As a result a stalemate lasted years until the Spaniards agreed to Yanga's terms. In 1618 the treaty was signed, and by 1630, the town of San Lorenzo de los Negros de Cerralvo was established. The 21st century town of Yanga is located in Veracruz, Mexico.

Stetson Kennedy (1916 – 2011), author & activist, infiltrated the Ku Klux Klan during the 1940's. He supplied the secret codes and rituals of the KKK to the writers of the wildly popular Superman radio show. The show used this information in their plots, stunning KKK members and humiliating them across the nation.

The Cherokee Indians, who held African-Americans as chattel slaves, had as many as 4,600 African slaves by 1860. The Cherokees depended on the slaves to run interference between them and the European settlers; the enslaved interpreted and translated, and they labored on the farms and in the homes of their captors. On November 15, 1842, a group of more than 25 slaves from the Joseph Vann plantation locked their masters and overseers in their homes and cabins while they slept. The enslaved stole ammunition, food, supplies, and whatever else they needed and headed toward Mexico, where slavery was illegal. The enslaved were not home free, however; they did have to fight. They were able to fight and kill the slave hunters who pursued them.

Florynce "Flo" Kennedy (1916-2000) was born in Kansas City, Missouri. Kennedy graduated at the top of her class at Lincoln High School, after which she and her sisters went into the millinery business. In 1942, after the death of her mother, Kennedy left Kansas and moved to Harlem with her sister Grayce. She began attending Columbia University in 1944, and graduated in 1949, but when she applied to the University's law school, she was refused admission. She threatened to sue because of the perceived racial discrimination; however, she was told that race was not the issue, gender was. She would not tolerate either slight and was admitted. Kennedy graduated from Columbia Law School in 1951. In 1956, she formed a legal partnership with the lawyer who had represented Billie Holiday when she was charged with drug offenses. Kennedy then came to represent Holiday's estate and also that of Charlie Parker. Kennedy played a significant role in many lawsuits supporting women and civil rights, attended all three Black Power conferences and represented H. Rap Brown, Assata Shakur and the Black Panthers. In 1973, Kennedy, along with Margaret Sloan-Hunter, founded the National Black Feminist Organization (NBFO), which also dealt with race and gender issues such as, reproductive rights and sterilization campaigns that were aimed at specific races.

Four women, members of Quinn Chapel African Methodist Episcopal Church in Chicago, Illinois, were known as "the big four" because they gave food, shelter, and supplies to runaway slaves. Their purpose was to supply the refugees with what they would need for the rest of their journey or to start a new life in Chicago. Of the four black women Emma J. Atkinson was the only name that was known. There were no records kept by the "Big Four" abolitionists, and little else is known about their work. In 1871, the chapel was destroyed in the Great Chicago Fire.

Robert Smalls (1839 - 1915), born in Beaufort, South Carolina, progressed from enslavement to a seat in the U.S. House of Representatives. During the Civil War, Smalls commandeered a Confederate ship and sailed it to Federal territory, freeing himself and many other slaves aboard the vessel. Hailed as a hero by the North, Smalls personally rallied President Lincoln to enlist African-American soldiers in the war. Lincoln agreed. Smalls served both the Navy and the Army as a civilian during the Civil War. He later founded the Republican Party of South Carolina and planted the seed for free and public school systems in the United States. Smalls served in the South Carolina state assembly and senate, and for five non-consecutive terms in the U.S. House of Representatives.

On Oct. 27, 1841, **Madison Washington,** an enslaved African who had gained his freedom but was re-enslaved when he returned to Virginia to free his wife, instituted what has been called, "the most successful slave revolt in U.S. history." One hundred twenty-eight enslaved persons were freed when they relocated to Nassau, Bahamas. The vessel ship, the *Creole* sailed from Richmond, Va., with 135 enslaved Africans, bound for New Orleans. During the trip, Washington and several other African men unshackled themselves, and quickly overcame the crew in the surprise attack. Washington and the men clubbed some of crewmembers to death and held the rest of them captive. The African men at first demanded to be taken to Liberia, W. Africa, but they did not have enough supplies to make that trip; they settled instead for a place under English rule. England had abolished slavery by this time. The Creole later arrived at Nassau, New Providence, where they were all set free by British authorities.

Osborne Perry Anderson (1830 - 1872) was one of the five African American men in John Brown's company when they raided the Federal Arsenal at Harpers Ferry, West Virginia, in October 1859. Anderson was a free man and attended Oberlin College.

On October 16, 1859, Anderson participated in the raid but was among the five followers of Brown, and the only African American, who escaped capture when U.S. Marines attacked the Arsenal to stop the raid. In 1864, five years after the Harpers Ferry Raid, Anderson enlisted in the Union Army, serving as a recruitment officer in Indiana and Arkansas.

On Thursday, June 29, 1820, at 3:00 P.M., nineteen years before the "Amistad" incident, 283 African slaves (two dead and 281 in chains) were aboard a slave vessel named **"The Antelope"**, when the ship was boarded by federal authorities of the United States Treasury. Slave trade was illegal in the U.S. at this time, and the U.S. filed suit to claim the Africans so that they could be returned to Africa. Other countries, however, also laid claim to the Africans. After about 2,576 days of captivity and legal battle in the United States, the portion of the Africans who had been placed in U.S. custody were returned to Africa; those who remained were sold to American slave owners and the proceeds of the sales were given to Portuguese and Spanish claimants.

Wouldn't it be interesting to compare and contrast the amount of time and money that has been expended in tracking down, indicting and prosecuting Blacks for crimes they didn't commit and who have later been proved to be innocent, to the negligible amount that has probably been spent in trying to find murderers of innocent black people. Somehow it seems that the trail on these latter perpetrators of injustice always goes "cold." Mo

HISTORIC PLACES

Thought to be the oldest town incorporated by African Americans in the United States, **Brooklyn "Lovejoy" Illinois** was founded by Priscilla and John Baltimore and a group of seven other families in the early 1820s. Lovejoy is located two miles north of East St. Louis, Missouri and three miles northeast of downtown St. Louis. Its location on the Mississippi River across from St. Louis was strategic in helping its citizens gain economic freedom as they pursued careers as brick masons, coopers, boatmen and carpenters. Despite its auspicious beginning, Lovejoy was not the "home of the free" because of Illinois' Black Laws that were established when the state joined the Union in 1819. These laws restricted the occupations of the Black citizens and forbade voting for Blacks.

Weeksville, a community founded in 1838 by ex-slave James Week, in the Ninth Ward of central Brooklyn, quickly became a thriving Black community. Becoming the second largest pre-Civil War community by 1850, Weeksville was a place where Black professionals, doctors, and entrepreneurs, could practice and build up a clientele. Additionally, Weeksville saw the rise of one of the country's first Black newspapers--*The Freedman's Torchlight*. The community existed until the 1930s.

Isaiah Montgomery and eleven other pioneers founded **Mound Bayou**, an all-black town in the Yazoo Delta in Northwest, MS, in 1887. Mound Bayou stood on land purchased from the Louisville, New Orleans and Texas Railroad (L, NO & T), and it served as an agent for this railroad. Isaiah Montgomery became the mayor of Mound Bayou and worked closely with Booker T. Washington. Mayor Montgomery also shared Booker T's philosophy that vocational education in scientific agriculture was a sure path for the economic survival of the Community. The Mound Bayou community thrived until the period of The Great Migration, during which cotton prices fell, Booker T passed away, and Blacks left the south in large numbers to move to northern cities. The community does, however, still exist today.

Oak Bluffs, on Martha's Vineyard, part of the Cape Cod islands in Massachusetts, is home to the Inkwell beach. The Inkwell was negatively named by local whites to designate it as the beach where Blacks frequented. Currently this name is used with pride by the many African Americans who visit Martha's Vineyard and make pilgrimages to the Inkwell. Some of the current African Americans homeowners are descendants of the employees of the white families who flocked to the island. Oak Bluffs' Black population increased during the mid- twentieth century when houses could be purchased for reasonable prices. Presently, most of the homes purchased during that period are worth 15 to 20 times the price paid for them, thus making Oak Bluffs one of the wealthiest Black resort towns in the U.S.

Throughout the United States, towns such as Mound Bayou and Weeksville existed--particularly during the southern Jim Crow era. I lived a few years in such a town in New Jersey--a town created by Blacks escaping the sharecropping misery of the South. This town, even during the 60s retained its southern essence--dirt roads, little one-story houses--one I visited often that still used a wood-burning stove to cook. A couple of little churches, a grocery store where the owner made his own sausage, a pool hall and a community center, and a touch of the "benevolent" government, a housing project, all donned the landscape of this town. I lived there just after integration made it okay to go to clubs and enter-tainment establishments in the cities, but I arrived before the town lost its unique flavor, its insularity, its safety...Mo

MILITARY

During WWII, the Women's Army Corps was originally known as the **Women's Army Auxiliary Corps**, and Charity Adams Earley (1918-2002) was the first African American woman to be an officer in this corps. This corps officially became the Women's Army Corps in 1943. In 1944, Earley, was given an overseas assignment, and along with another officer, went to Scotland to meet her troops. As maintaining the morale of her troops was an integral part of her job, she, with the help of other officers, made it possible for African American hair products and African American salons to become available for her troops. By the end of the war, Earley was the highest ranking African American in the army. In 1989, she published a book, One Woman's Army.

Frank E. Petersen (1932-2015) enlisted in the Navy in 1950. That was the beginning of a stellar career in the Navy and Marines. Petersen became the first African American to be named a naval aviator, the first to command a fighter squadron, a fighter air group, an air wing and a major base. Petersen, who held the honorary titles of Silver Hawk and Grey Eagle, was known among his friends and associates as a leader and gentleman.

Roscoe Robinson, Jr., (1928-1993) a West Point graduate, became the US Army's first African American four-star general. During his career he received the Bronze Star for his actions in the Korean War. For his Vietnam service he received the Legion of Merit, the Distinguished Flying Cross, 11 Air Medals and two Silver Stars.

Currently the second highest-ranking officer in the **U.S. Navy, Admiral Michelle Janine Howard** was attracted to military life when, as a child, she traveled the world as a child of a military man. Howard's military life began with admission to the Naval Academy in 1978, one of seven black women in the class of 1,363 students. She graduated from the Academy in 1982 and subsequently earned a master's degree from the U.S. Army's Command & General Staff College at Ft. Leavenworth, KS. Howard served as commander of an amphibious squadron that aided in the relief of the Indian Ocean tsunami of 2004. She is the first African American woman to lead a US Navy battle group, the Expeditionary Strike Group Two--a flotilla which performed anti-piracy operations in the Indian Ocean. Sailors under her command aided in the rescue of Captain Richard Phillips who had been held hostage by Somali pirates.

MARC - Despite the giant hole that exists in American history regarding Blacks' service in the military, we have fought valiantly in every conflict going back to before the country was formed. Blacks in the military have faced the unenviable task of having to fight the enemy at war and the enemy at home, oftentimes risking their lives for a country that treated captured enemy combatants better than themselves.

Dorie Miller (1919-1943) was assigned to the mess hall as an attendant when he joined the navy in 1939. He did not receive training in machine gun use, as that kind of training was usually not available to African Americans. Despite his lack of readiness for combat, Miller jumped into action when the Japanese attacked U.S. ships in 1941. He pulled a captain and several of his crewmates to safety; then, he returned to the bridge, grabbed an antiaircraft gun and began firing at Japanese planes. He is credited with having shot down two Japanese warplanes, but he may have shot down as many as six. The navy did not acknowledge his heroism until the Black press pressured them, and in 1942, he was awarded the third highest medal in the navy, the Navy Cross. He was killed in action when USS *Liscome Bay* was sunk by a Japanese submarine during the Battle of Makin.

Charles Young (1864-1922), son of slaves, enjoyed many "firsts" in his life. Although he was not the first African American to graduate from West Point Academy, despite bigotry, harassment, and racial slurs, he was the third to endure. Leaving the Academy with the rank of Second Lieutenant, Young was first assigned to the Tenth U.S. Cavalry regiment, and then reassigned to the Ninth U.S. Cavalry regiment. He subsequently served chiefly with Black troops. Young served for five years then left the military to become a professor at Wilberforce University, where he became good friends with W.E.B. DuBois. During the Spanish American War, Young rejoined the military with the rank of major and was in charge of the cavalry as they participated in the famous charge up San Juan Hill in Cuba. Young eventually attained the honor of being the first African American promoted to the rank of Colonel in the Army, and later became the first African American to be appointed as military attaché. He was also the first African American superintendent of a National Park, and he remained the highest ranking African American in the regular army until his death.

John C. Robinson (1903-1954), Florida born, Mississippi raised, became fascinated with airplanes early in his life. Not only did he want to fly, but he also wanted to know the mechanics of the plane. His road to mechanic status was circuitous and laborious. He was unable to obtain past a tenth-grade education in his city of Gulfport, in Mississippi; however, he was allowed to enroll in Tuskegee Institute to study automobile mechanics. After graduating from Tuskegee, Robinson tried unsuccessfully to obtain a job in auto mechanics, lamenting the fact that he could have been hired in an establishment as a gas-attendant or a janitor, but not an engine man. Ultimately, he found work in Detroit, MI, where he was promoted to a full mechanic. He tried several times to enroll in the Curtiss-Wright School of Aviation in Chicago to further his studies, but he was denied every time that he applied. He, like so many others before and after him, had to get a "backdoor" education. He became a janitor at Curtiss-Wright and monitored the classes until he was permitted to enroll, becoming the first black student at the school.

Robinson and a friend formed the Challenger Air Pilots Association for African Americans, hoping to help others like himself who had the yen for flying. To that end, Robinson also founded the John Robinson School of Aviation in Illinois and convinced his alma mater Tuskegee Institute to open an aviation school. In 1935, Robinson, volunteered to fly Ethiopian planes in their fight against Italy. Robinson became the commander of the Ethiopian Air Force. As a result of his desire to be recognized as able and knowledgeable enough to fly a plane and having to leave his country to do so, Robinson is credited with the U.S. finally allowing African

Americans to enlist in the Army Air Corps. He is also sometimes referred to as the Father of the Tuskegee Airmen.

During WWII, **Black troops at Ft. Benning, GA**, who were charged with clean-up duty and cooking, were not permitted to use the Post on the base; white troops used the Post--even German prisoners of war were permitted access to the Post. The Black troops watched the white troops training to be paratroopers, but as close as the Black enlistees came to that duty was cleaning the area where the white troops trained. Of course their morale was low.

Their commanding officer, acting first sergeant Walter Morris, took a risk and started training his men on the same training ground that they had cleaned after the white troops had finished for the day. The African American troops earned the attention of the commanding general who, in 1943, placed Sergeant Morris in charge of the 555th Parachute Infantry Company, coming to be known as the Triple Nickels. After graduation, the Triple Nickels expected to be assigned to duty in Europe, supporting the white troops, but those in charge thought that rather than fighting the enemy, the blacks and whites would fight each other. Instead, the Triple Nickels became smokejumpers, assigned to the Forest Service as part of Operation US Firefly, a joint civilian-military effort to counteract wildfires ignited by Japanese incendiary devices. Altogether the Triple Nickels had 36 fire missions.

After running away from his home in Georgia at the age of 11, where he witnessed his father's near fatal brush with lynching, **Eugene Jacques Bullard** (1895-1961) began his action-packed life. This journey would take him from a life with the gypsies in Atlanta to Aberdeen, Scotland, and other parts of Europe where he supported himself by being a fighter; to France where he joined the French Foreign Legion. Bullard gained renown as a pilot for flying into dangerous situations and became known as the "black swallow of death." When the United States entered WWI, Bullard and other expatriates tried to join the US Army, but they were denied on the basis of race. The United States, in fact, wanted France to discharge all of the African Americans from their military and to support the U.S. in their refusal to allow African Americans to serve in the military. Bullard was awarded 15 French war medals, and when Charles DeGaulle, the French president, came to the U.S. in 1960, he made a special trip to NYC see and embrace Bullard.

Aaron Anderson or Sanderson (1811 - 1896) joined the Navy at an age when most men retire from active duty. During the Civil War, Anderson or Sanderson kept the Confederate troops from getting supplies. During one incident, shortly before the war ended, Anderson/Sanderson was in a group that was being fired upon, but he managed to fire a howitzer until his entire group was safely out of the way. For his actions, he was awarded the Medal of Honor, military's highest honor.

Born **Dovey Mae Johnson** on April 17, 1914, in Charlotte, North Carolina, Dovey Johnson Roundtree is an African American civil rights activist, attorney, and ordained minister who won the 1955 Interstate Commission case on segregated bus terminals.

Johnson attended Spelman College from 1934 to 1938 and then briefly taught school in South Carolina before moving to Washington, D.C., to seek employment in the burgeoning World War II defense industry.

Because of her college education, Ms. Johnson was instead selected by Mary McLeod Bethune to be among the forty African American women who would become the first to train as officers in the newly formed Women's Army Auxiliary Corps.

I remember hearing my uncle, my friend's father, and even one of my own friends relate stories of the humiliation that they suffered in the armed forces—during World War II and after, through the sixties. All three of these independent family men were relegated to the kitchen where they peeled piles of potatoes, I am sure. What happened to their dreams of learning a trade? Sure they were issued uniforms, and they could have their pictures taken and hear folks "ooh and ah" about how "fine" they were. Deep down inside, though, they knew that it was just another one of those "bounced" checks that this country wrote—"Insufficient respect, return these men to the kitchen." **Mo**

POLITICS

A Washingtonian, **Robert C. Weaver** (1907-1997) became the first African American appointed to the cabinet. He served as the Secretary of the Dept. of Housing and Urban Development from 1966-1968. This position, however, was the pinnacle of Weaver's achievements. He had a long and distinguished career in government service prior to his cabinet position, including special assistant for the Housing Authority, Department of the Interior's first Black adviser on racial problems, and Chicago's executive director of the Mayor's Committee on Race and Relations. Weaver also served as chairman of the NAACP and authored several books.

Mifflin Wistar Gibbs (1823 - 1915) thought that he would partake of the riches to be found on the west coast of the United States during the Gold Rush. After arriving in California as a young man, he became disillusioned by the discriminatory laws and he, along with several other African Americans, moved to Victoria, British Columbia. Once the Civil War was over and during the brief period of Reconstruction, Gibbs returned to the United States and settled in Little Rock, Arkansas, where he became the first Black judge elected in the US. In 1897, Gibbs was appointed as American consul to Madagascar.

Oscar Stanton DePriest (1871-1951) was a Chicago politician; however, unlike many other famous African American Chicagoans, DePriest was a Republican, not a Democrat. He represented Illinois in the House of Representatives from 1929-1935, and was the first African American elected to Congress from outside the southern states. DePriest, who had made a name and place for himself in Chicago politics, did not find that Washington, DC (a still-segregated city) was equally as accepting. Some of his fellow representatives from the South refused to allow their offices to be situated next to his. Also, when his wife Jessie Williams DePriest was not invited to tea at the White House with the wives of other representatives, DePriest publicized the snub, and Louise Hoover recapitulated and invited Mrs. DePriest. DePriest felt that he was elected in the same manner as his white counterparts, and he should be afforded the same respect as they.

Edward Joseph Perkins (1928 -) a Louisiana native has had a stellar career. After 13 years in the Foreign Service, Perkins was appointed ambassador of Liberia by Pres. Ronald Reagan, followed quickly by an appointment as ambassador to South Africa. After serving in South Africa, Ambassador Perkins returned to the U.S. to become the first African American Director General of the Foreign Service. President George H.W. Bush appointed him as U.S. Permanent Representative to the United Nations with Ambassador as his title. Pres. Bill Clinton appointed him as ambassador to Australia. Mr. Perkins, an active member of Kappa Alpha Psi fraternity, holds the highest award that Kappa awards its members, the Laurel Wreath award.

Elizabeth Spurlock Sampson (1898 - 1979), born in Pittsburgh, PA, first sought a career in social work. While studying at the NY School of Social Work, one of her instructors noticed that she excelled at criminology. This instructor, George Kirchwey, suggested that she pursue a law degree. Ms. Sampson obtained a degree in law from John Marshall School of Law and a Master's Degree in Law from Loyola University in 1927, becoming the first woman to receive a law degree from that university. Sampson became active in community organizations in Chicago and in local politics, serving as Assistant State's Attorney in Cook County in 1947. From 1950 to 1953, Sampson served as a UN delegate, becoming the first Black woman to be named to that position.

William Allison Davis (1902 - 1983) was raised in Washington, DC, and was class valedictorian of his Dunbar High School graduating class. Following high school graduation, Davis graduated summa cum laude from Williams College where he earned his bachelor's degree; then, he earned a master's degree in English from Harvard in 1925. After relocating to Virginia, Davis used his credentials to teach English to Black children living in rural areas. Davis was interested in and troubled by the lower intelligence scores attributed to Black students. His view was that the scores did not confirm lower intelligence; rather, they confirmed that the questions asked were culturally biased. Following the completion of his Ph.D. in anthropology, he performed an extensive study of standardized intelligence testing, the results of which showed that the lower two-thirds of the socioeconomic spectrum were unfairly affected by lower test scores. His research in this area ultimately led to another test choice, the Davis-Ellis Intelligence Test--a test that was free of social bias. Davis served on the Commission on Civil Rights under Presidents Johnson and Nixon and on the White House Task Force for the Gifted in 1968.

Oscar J. Dunn is best remembered as Louisiana's first Black Lieutenant Governor, serving from 1868 to 1871. As a young man, Oscar Dunn was a slave who fled bondage and purchased his freedom. Before obtaining his freedom, Dunn educated himself by reading letters and learned the art of public speaking from actors who stayed at his mother's lodging establishment. As a child Dunn worked as an apprentice plasterer, and as a young adult, he was a music teacher.

During the Civil War, Dunn fought in the Union Army for the 1st Louisiana Native Guard, rising from Private to Captain. The Native Guards were one of the first all-black regiments to fight for the Union during the Civil War (1861-1865).

Dunn's career as a public official unofficially began in December 1864. At mass meetings in New Orleans, he emerged as one of a handful of powerful radical voices demanding Black legal equality and suffrage in Louisiana's new state government.

Patricia Roberts Harris, (1924 - 1985) the first African American U.S. Ambassador was named permanent chairman of the Democratic National Convention. She was later appointed Secretary of Health and Human Services and Secretary of Housing and Urban development.

Patricia Roberts Harris was born in Mattoon, Illinois. She excelled academically and received a scholarship to Howard University. During her time at Howard, Roberts was elected Phi Beta Kappa and graduated Summa Cum Laude in 1945. While she was in college Roberts participated in civil rights protests in Washington, D.C. In 1943, she took part in one of the earliest student sit-ins at a whites-only cafeteria.

And now we have made it all the way to White House, with class and smarts and dignity—standing on the shoulders of the aforementioned who paved the way. Interestingly enough, most of our presidents have been English, with a few Irish and Scottish sprinkled in. One president has been of German descent, and only one Catholic has been in residence at 1500 Pennsylvania Ave. The true fact is that the United States is no longer a homogeneously populated country. It is quite difficult to hide the "brown" people when it comes time to take pictures. We are here, and here we will stay—on Capitol Hill, in the State Houses and in the White House...Mo

SCIENCE

Ola Orekunrin was born in Nigeria in either 1986 or 1987. She began college in the UK at age 15 and became a medical doctor at 21, all the while supporting herself by working. After experiencing a grave emergency with her younger sister who suffered from sickle cell disease and who was visiting in Nigeria and unable to get air transportation that could move her to hospital where she could be treated, Orekunrin founded The Flying Doctors. Currently, Orekunrin's company, the first air ambulance service in West Africa, uses a fleet of helicopters and planes to lift critically ill patients from remote areas to health care facilities where they can be helped.

Ed Dwight, Jr. was born in Chicago in 1933. He became the first African American candidate for astronaut in the agency now known as NASA when Whitney Young, Jr. suggested it to President John F. Kennedy. Unfortunately, Pres. Kennedy was assassinated before Dwight actually experienced any space travel, and Dwight, enduring an increasingly hostile, racial atmosphere resigned from the agency.

Jaylen Bledsoe, born in St. Louis, Missouri, created his own tech company when he was just 13 years old in 2011. In just two years, his company, Bledsoe Technologies was worth millions. Jaylen's company does web design and other forms of IT consulting for companies located mainly in the Midwest.

Mark Dean, born in Jefferson City, Tennessee, in 1957, is a computer scientist and engineer who has worked at IBM. He has developed several landmark technologies including the PC monitor and the first gigahertz chip. He also holds three of IBM's original nine patents and he invented the Industry Standard Architecture system bus that allows for computer plug-ins.

MARC - Technology has seemed to have taken over the world, but somehow Blacks have been missing from the narrative of how that came to be. In spite of a country that made it all but impossible for Blacks to not only study the sciences but also apply the knowledge once it was acquired, Blacks have been part of inventions, explorations, and discoveries from the beginning of America.

Rebecca Davis Lee Crumpler was born free in Delaware in 1831, and died in Hyde Park, NY, in 1895. It was commonly thought that Dr. Rebecca Cole was the first black female physician, but research has shown that Dr. Crumpler enrolled in the New England Female Medical College in 1860 and was awarded her medical degree from the same. She was subject to intense racism by male doctors, druggists, and average citizens, some of whom made the comment that the M.D. after her name stood for "mule driver." Anxious to provide medical care for newly freed people, Dr. Crumpler moved to Richmond, Virginia, and worked with Freedmen's Bureau after the Civil War ended in 1865.

Katherine G. Johnson's interest in mathematics propelled her from West Virginia to NASA. Born in White Sulfur Springs, WV, in 1918, Ms. Johnson attended West Virginia State College, where she studied under the tutelage of Dr. W.W. Schiefflin Claytor, the third African American in the United States to earn a Ph.D. degree in mathematics. Dr. Claytor tailor-made a course in analytic geometry for Ms. Johnson. In 1938, Katherine became the first African American woman to desegregate the graduate school at West Virginia University in Morgantown.

Ms. Johnson first joined the National Advisory Committee for Aeronautics, a part of the Langley Research Center in 1953. NACA became NASA in 1958, and as a NASA employee in the Spacecraft Controls Branch, Ms. Johnson calculated the flight trajectory for Alan Shepard, the first American to go into space in 1959. Johnson verified the mathematics that supported John Glenn's orbit around the Earth in 1962, and calculated the flight trajectory for Apollo 11's 1969 flight to the moon. On November 16, 2015, President Barack Obama included Johnson on a list of 17 Americans to be awarded the Presidential Medal of Freedom in 2015. . This occurred on the 55th anniversary of Alan Shepard's historic rocket launch and splashdown, which Johnson helped make possible. Ms. Johnson is one of the women written about by Margot Lee Shetterly in her book *Hidden Figures*, and seen on the big screen in a hit movie of the same name.

Clarence "Skip" Ellis was born on May 11, 1943, in Chicago, Illinois. Dr. Ellis escaped the fate that poverty and violence often wreaks upon many and became the first African American to earn a Ph.D in computer science. Skip Ellis took a job watching a computer in 1958, and went on to earn his Master's and Ph.D from the University of Illinois. He worked for some of the most well known companies and universities in the world, including: MIT, Stanford, the University of Texas, Bell Telephone Labs, IBM, and Xerox. Dr. Ellis is considered a pioneer in the field of observational transformation that is found in a variety of computer applications such as Apache Wave and Google Docs. In 2009, he became an emeritus professor at the University of Colorado, Boulder. In 2013, Ellis won a Fulbright Scholarship to teach and perform research in the computer science department at Ashesi University.

An African slave who was shipped to America in 1724, **Thomas Fuller** astonished people with his mathematical ability. When antislavery campaigners discovered him, they used him as proof of their assertion that blacks are not inferior to whites. Two Pennsylvania gentlemen, who were visiting Alexandria, met Fuller when he was about 70 and asked him two questions. First, they asked him how many seconds there were in a year and a half, and he answered in about two minutes, 47,304,000. Secondly, they asked him how many seconds a man has lived who is 70 years, 17 days and 12 hours old, and he answered in a minute and a half 2,210,500,800. Because one of the men was working out the problems on paper, and his calculations indicated that the answer was a smaller number than Fuller had stated, he told Fuller that he was wrong. Fuller corrected the man's calculations by saying that the man had forgotten to figure in the leap year. When the man corrected his work, his sum matched Fuller's.

Dr. Helen O. Dickens (1909 - 2002), the daughter of former enslaved became the first African American woman admitted to the American College of Surgeons. An Ohio native, Dr. Dickens graduated from the University of Illinois School of Medicine, where she would often sit in the front of the class so that she could attempt to ignore racist comments and gestures made by some of her classmates. After a residency at Harlem Hospital, Dr. Dickens was certified by the American Board of Obstetrics and Gynecology. Dr. Dickens devoted her life to improving the physical health of women, particularly in the area of obstetrics and gynecology. She founded the Teen Clinic for school-age mothers in the inner city at the University of Pennsylvania Hospital in the late 1960s. This clinic not only provided medical services to teen mothers and their babies, but it also assisted them in finishing their education. The Helen O. Dickens Lifetime Achievement Award was established in her honor and is given to outstanding people who have a long history of service to women of color in the Delaware Valley and Penn communities.

As late as June of 1973, two impoverished girls, **Minnie Lee Relf,** 14 years old, and her mentally disabled sister, Mary Alice, 12 years old were sterilized, involuntarily. Their mother signed for the girls to receive birth control injections at the request of personnel from the Montgomery Community Action Agency in Montgomery, Alabama, but because these injections had been discontinued (as a result of carcinogenic effect on farm animals), federal funds were used to permanently sterilize the girls. The Southern Poverty Law Center helped the family to become a part of a class action suit that questioned the practice of women on Medicaid being coerced into sterilization and federal funds being used to accomplish this end. This case was instrumental in guidelines being set for the use of federal funds in sterilization procedures.

From the hoe in the field to the scalpel in the OR, **Dr. Matilda Evans** (1872 - 1935) made great strides in her 63 years. After graduating from Women's Medical College in Philadelphia, in 1897, Dr. Evans returned to South Carolina and set up practice, becoming the first African American female to practice medicine in that state. Evans had a special concern for black children. Dr. Evans believed that healthcare should be a citizenship right and governmental responsibility, much like education. She strongly advocated public health care and petitioned the State Board of Health of South Carolina to give her free vaccines for black children. In 1916, Evans created the Negro Health Association of South Carolina and in 1918, she volunteered in the Medical Service Corps of the United States Army during World War I. In 1922, Dr. Evans became the only black woman to be president of a state medical society, when she became president of the South Carolina's Palmetto Medical Association. Dr. Evans was active in her community, always advocating for children. Eventually she adopted seven children and fostered many more.

Two generations out of slavery, **Percy Julian** (1899-1975) of Montgomery, Alabama, was unable to attend high school in his hometown because he was black, so he was forced to attend a teacher training school. From there he went on to graduate Phi Beta Kappa and first in his class from DePauw University in Green Castle, Indiana. Julian continued his education at Harvard University where he became the first African American to obtain a master's degree in Chemistry. Because Harvard would not admit him to its PhD program, Julian enrolled at the University of Vienna and was able to earn his PhD. Dr. Julian's research and work led to a widely used treatment for glaucoma. In addition, Dr. Julian found a way to create synthetic progesterone, a drug used in hormone replacement therapy and to prevent uterine cancer. Additionally, he developed a way to create synthetic cortisone, a "wonder" drug for arthritis treatment.

The Science career that I knew growing up was that of nursing; in fact, it was my choice for career, originally. Healthcare careers were not as diverse as they now are, and very few, African American men or women considered engineering. I now have the opportunity to teach all subjects, including science, to my class of elementary students, and I must say that science today is awesome! Hands on science in the elementary school invites our Black students into the world of Science--research, immunology, biochemistry, genetics, electrical engineering, environmental engineering--and so many more careers. Natural curiosity is no longer thwarted by dull textbooks and boring language; rather, it is encouraged and welcomed. Viva la difference! Mo

SPORTS

Playing first for the San Francisco Lions, then the Black Pelicans, the New Orleans Creoles, the Indianapolis Clowns and finally the Kansas City Monarchs, **Toni Stone** (1921-1996) aka Marcenia Lyle Alberga was the first of three women to play in the Negro Baseball League. Not only did Stone have to endure discrimination from the crowds because she was a woman, but sometimes she also had to suffer the disdain from her fellow players. Coupled with the laws that prevailed in the South during the time she was playing, life was not always easy for Toni Stone.

MARC - Blacks have excelled at sports at a far faster and more prosperous rate than any other area of American life, and Black sports heroes are revered throughout history. Blacks, however, still struggle with participating in management and ownership, where the real power lies, and have only recently cracked the old-boy networks that barred them from being able to make decisions in sports that affect more than themselves.

The first Black professional basketball team "**The Renaissance**" organized in Harlem, in 1923. They were known to their many fans and admirers as "The Rens, " and they've been called "the greatest basketball team you never heard of." In 1939, they became the first all-black professional team to win a world championship.

After several failed attempts to qualify for the US Olympic Track Team, **Vonetta Flowers** born in 1973, in Birmingham, Alabama, earned a gold medal as a brakewoman on the 2002 Winter Olympics bobsledding team.

Charlie Sifford, an Army veteran of the Battle of Okinawa, became the first Black person to win a major professional golf tournament, Long Beach Open, in 1957. Sifford began playing as a pro in the late 1940s, but he was relegated to the black players' tour and its meager purses as he competed well into his 30s. Only after the P.G.A. dropped its Caucasians-only rule in 1961, did he get a chance to go up against the golf world's best. He won the Greater Hartford Open in 1967 and the Los Angeles Open in 1969. He also won the United Golf Association's National Negro Open six times, and the PGA Seniors' Championship in 1975.

Sports is another subject that I heard about while being real quiet and letting my parents talk. They talked about how much fun they had attending games between teams in the Negro Baseball League in Philadelphia. This would happen in the early 1940s; they would walk to a neighborhood baseball diamond, sometimes bringing their own seats and always bringing their own snacks. They would "meet up" with a lot of friends and cheer their favorite team and players. The cost was minimal because no one had much money, but the fun was free. Entertainment--Black style--pre-integration. Mo